DMITRI
KABALEVSKY

30 PIECES FOR CHILDREN (Op. 27)

for Piano

Edited by Joseph Prostakoff

G. SCHIRMER, Inc.

DISTRIBUTED BY

HAL•LEONARD®
CORPORATION
7777 W. BLUEMOUND RD. P.O. BOX 13819 MILWAUKEE, WI 53213

Contents

1. Waltz Time 2
2. Ditty 3
3. Etude 4
4. At Night on the River 6
5. Playing Ball 7
6. Sad Story 9
7. Old Dance 10
8. Cradle Song 11
9. Little Fable 13
10. Clowning 14
11. Rondo 16
12. Toccatina 18
13. A Little Prank 20
14. Scherzo 23
15. March 25
16. Lyric Piece 27
17. Meadow Dance 29
18. Sonatina 30
19. War Dance 32
20. Fairy Tale 34
21. The Chase 36
22. The Tale 38
23. Snow Storm 41
24. Etude 45
25. Novelette 48
26. Etude 50
27. Dance 54
28. Caprice 56
29. Songs of the Cavalry 59
30. Dramatic Episode 62

Preface

Dmitri Kabalevsky writes for children with such a freshness of mood and such insight into pianistic problems that these piano pieces have just become "required repertoire" throughout the world.

This is the first time that the *complete* set of *Piano Pieces for Children, Op. 27* has been published in the United States. This publication is based on a new version, revised by the composer, in which a number of changes were made in the music.

Very little editing has been added to the original version — only a few directions which I thought might help the young performers. The original fingering is very bold, and even, provocative. Only rarely did I change it for a simpler one. A possible pedaling has been indicated in a few cases where the original version had none.

J.P.

Thirty Pieces for Children

Dmitri Kabalevsky, Op. 27
Edited by Joseph Prostakoff

1
Waltz Time

2
Ditty

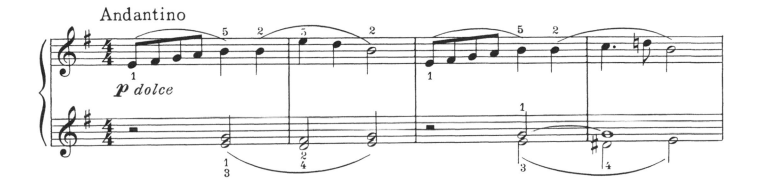

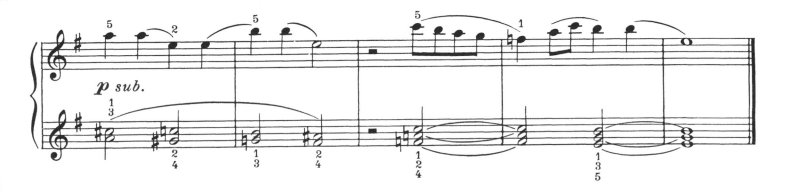

3
Etude

Allegro vivace

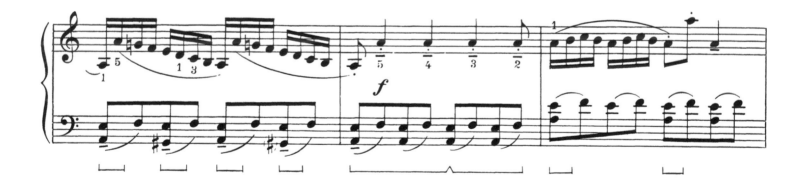

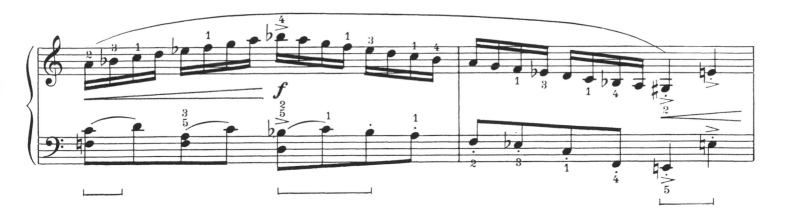

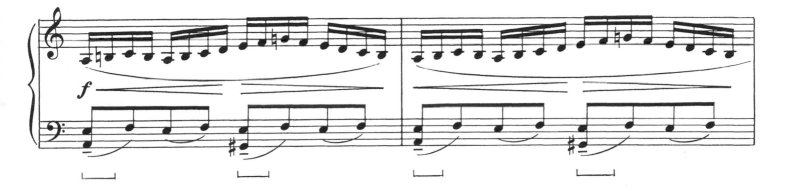

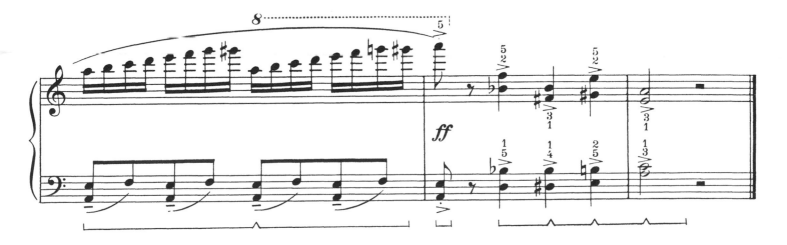

4
At Night on the River

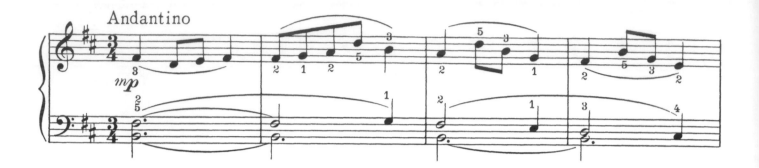

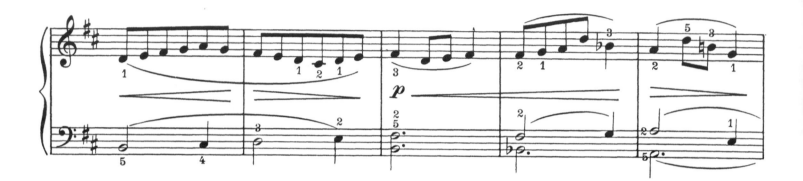

5
Playing Ball

Vivace leggero

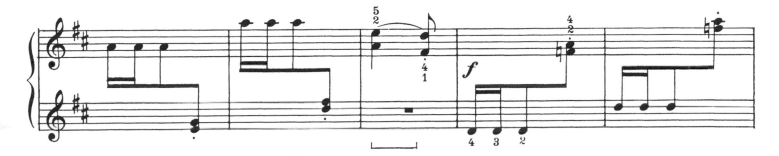

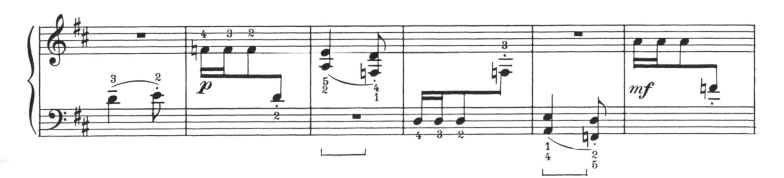

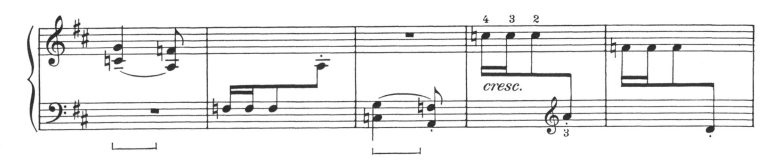

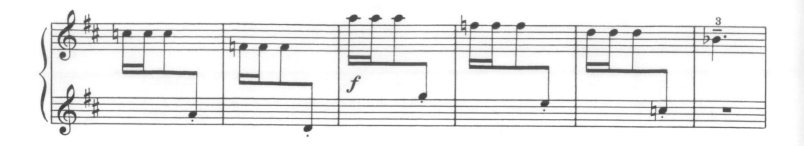

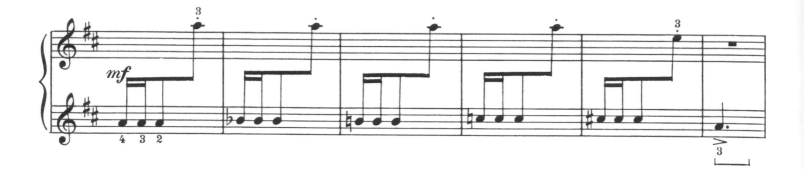

6
Sad Story

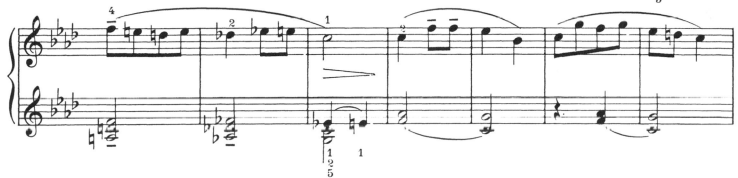

7
Old Dance

Tempo di Menuetto

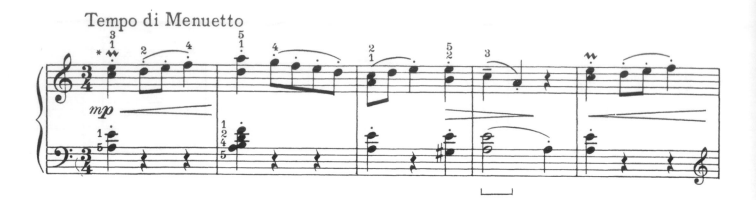

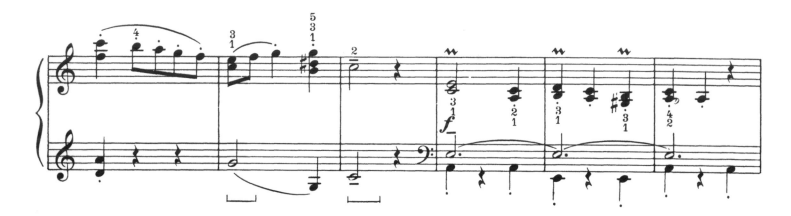

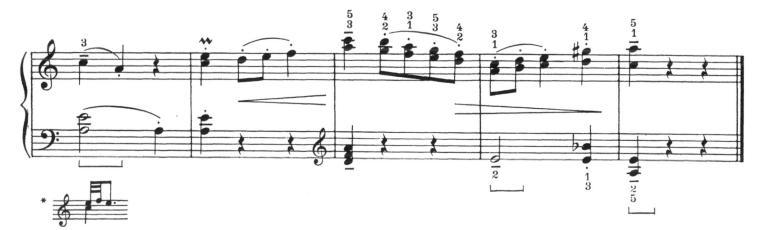

8
Cradle Song

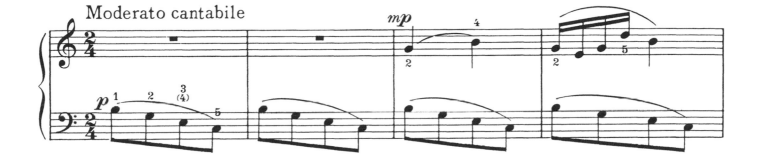

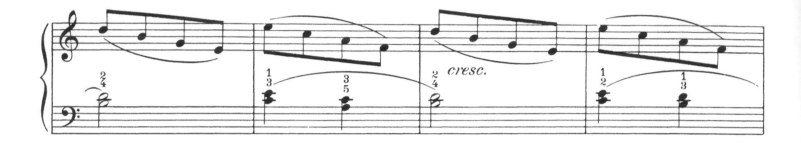

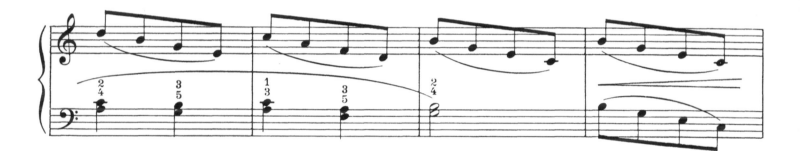

9
Little Fable

10
Clowning

Vivace

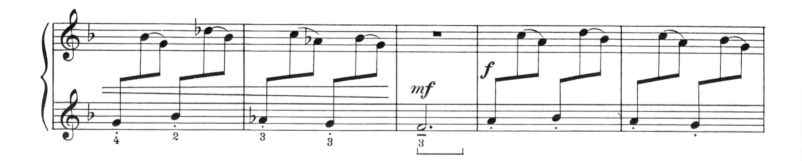

46334

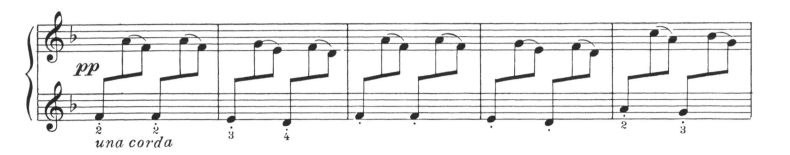

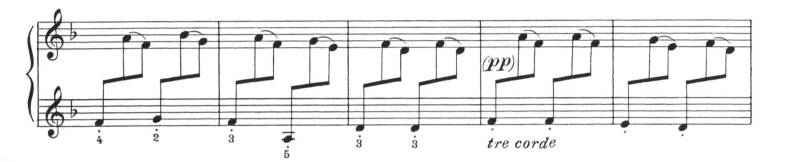

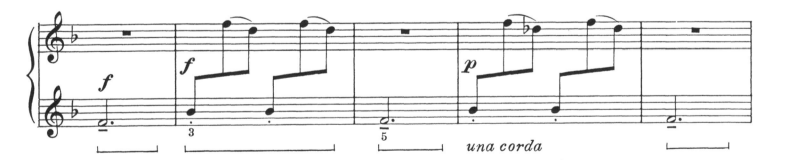

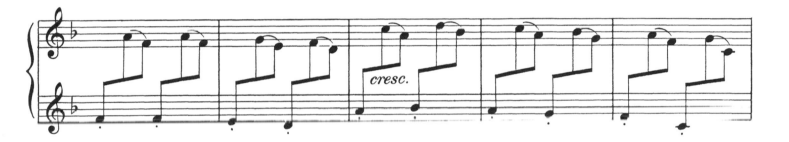

11
Rondo

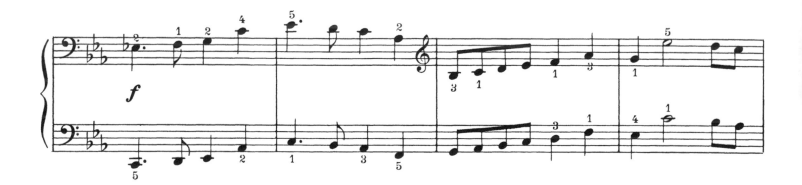

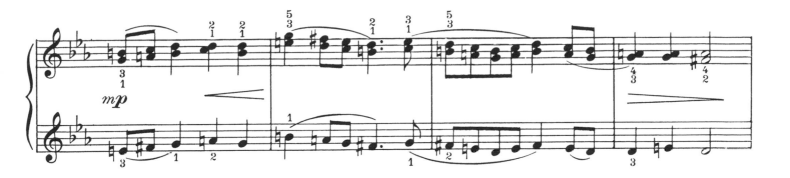

12
Toccatina

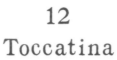

13
A Little Prank

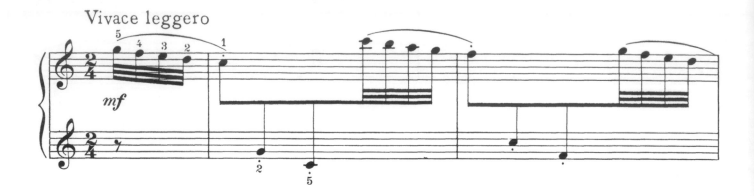

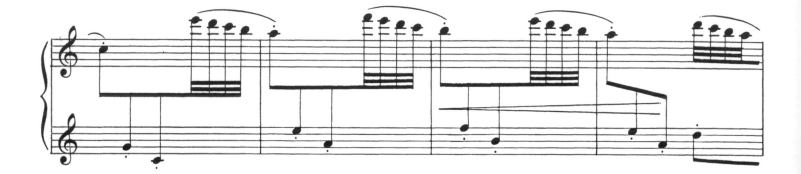

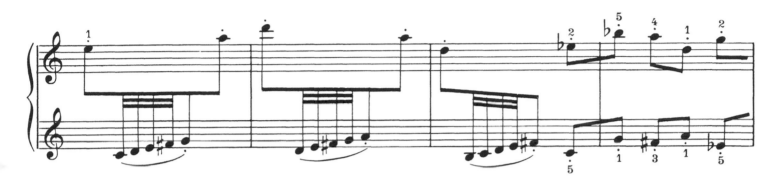

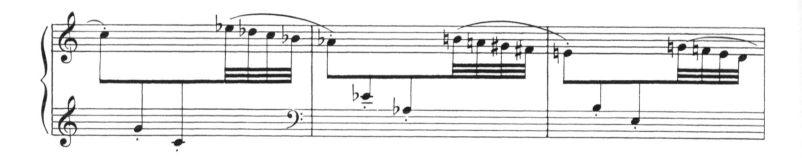

14
Scherzo

Allegro scherzando

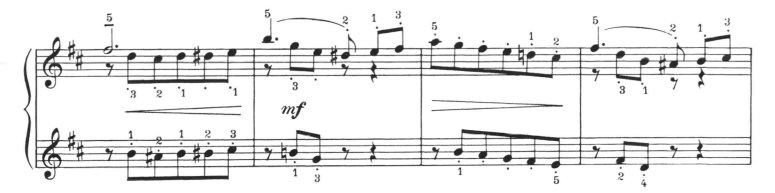

poco rit.   a tempo

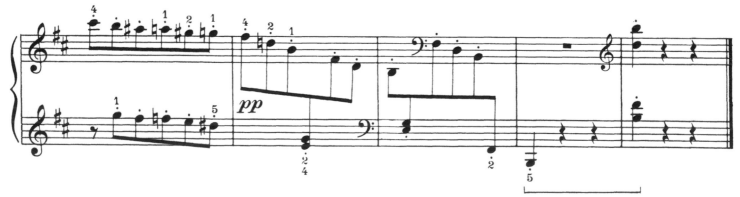

15
March

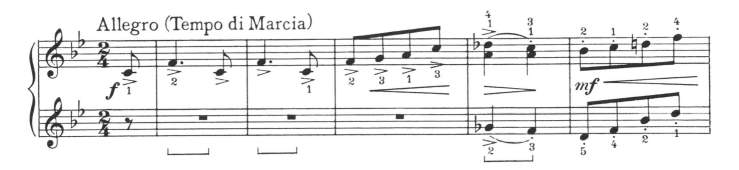

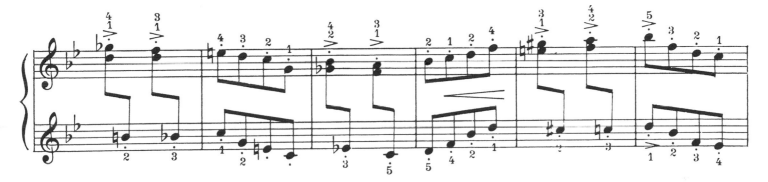

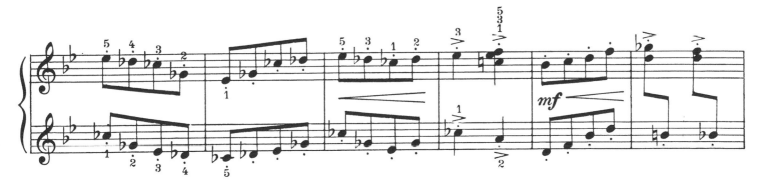

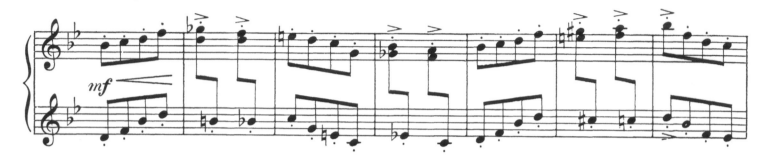

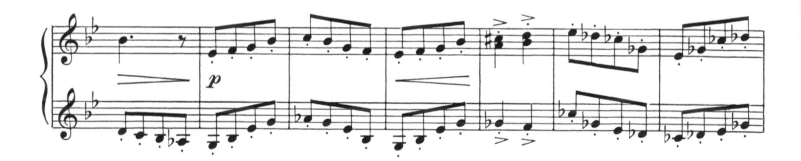

16
Lyric Piece

Andantino con moto

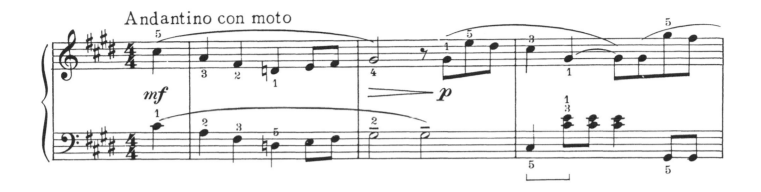

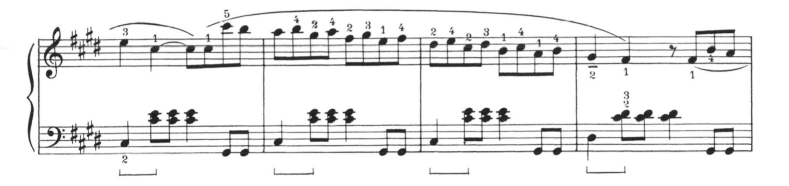

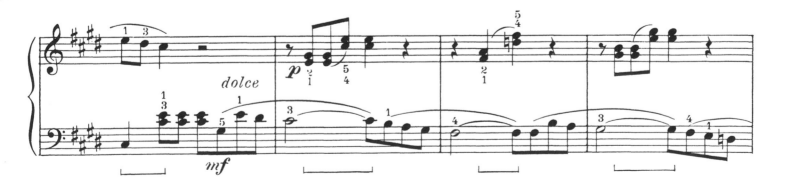

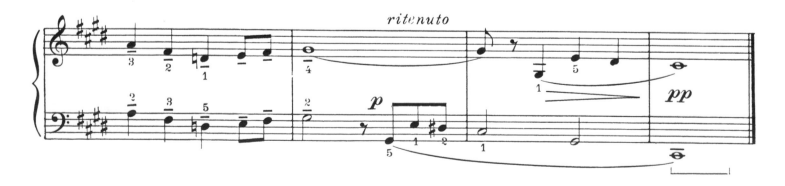

17
Meadow Dance

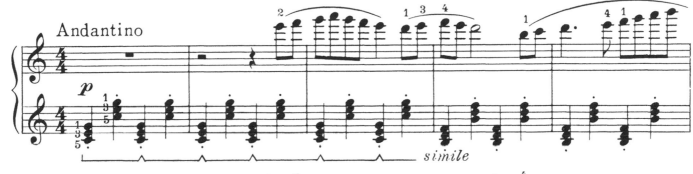

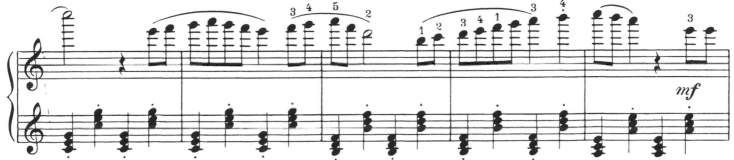

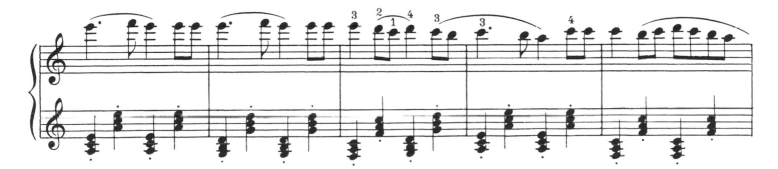

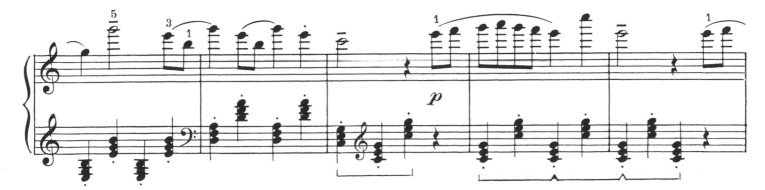

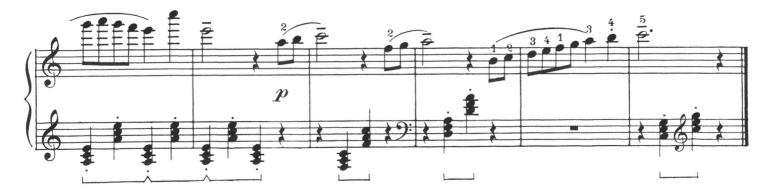

18
Sonatina

Allegretto

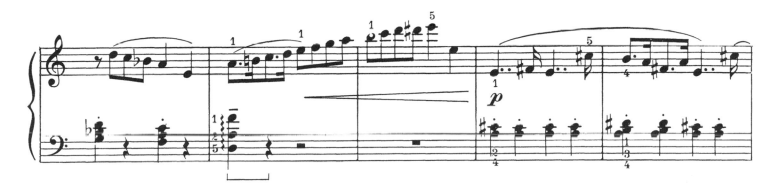

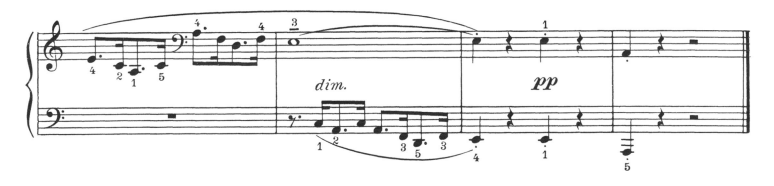

19
War Dance

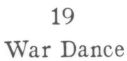

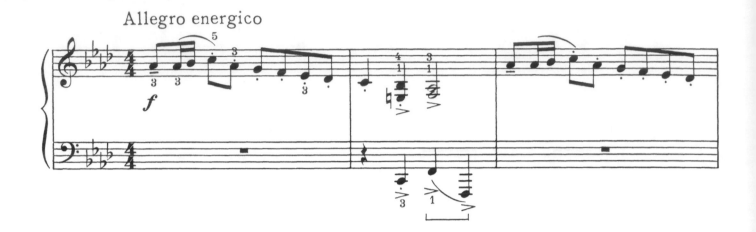

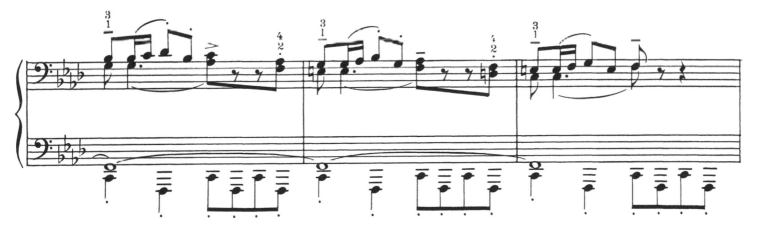
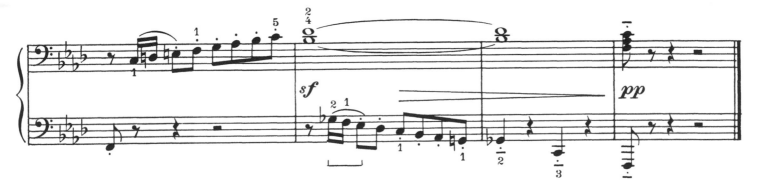

20
Fairy Tale

poco rit.   a tempo

pp poco a poco cresc.

poco rit.

46334

21
The Chase

Allegro moderato

22
A Tale

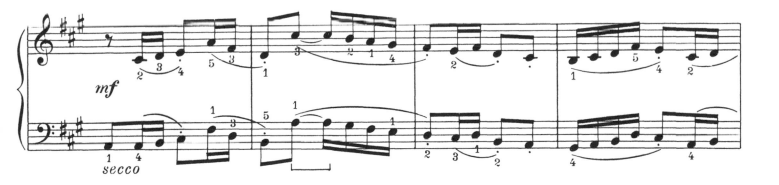

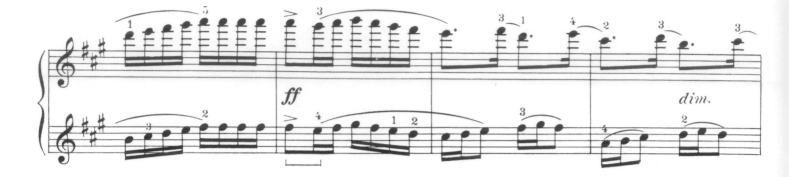

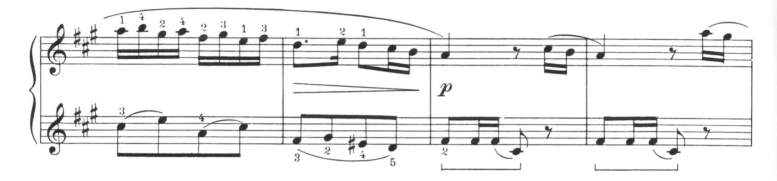

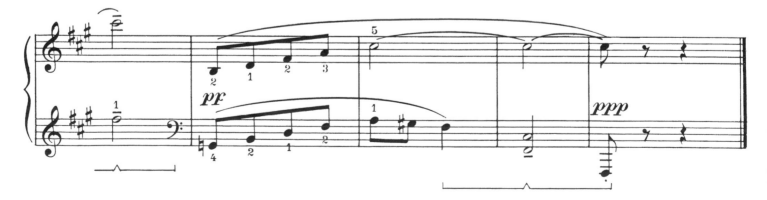

23
Snow Storm

24
Etude

Allegro marcato

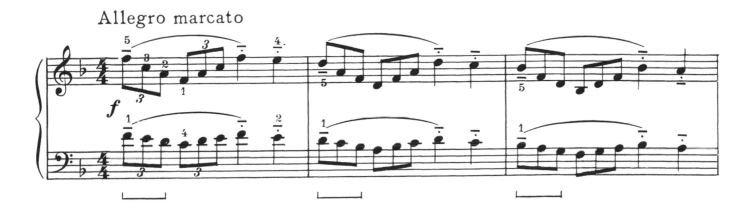

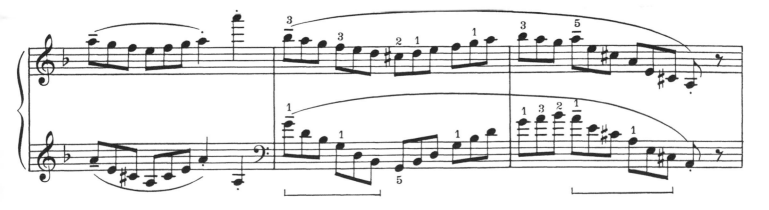

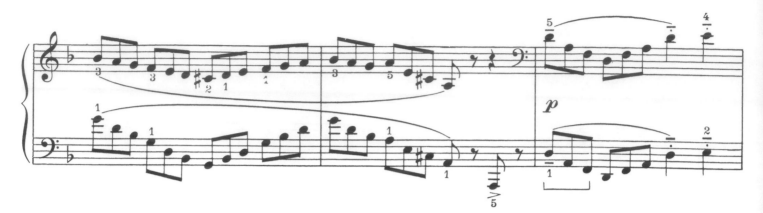

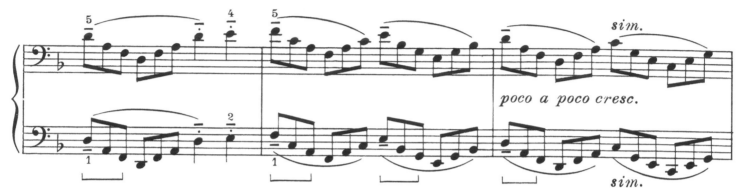

25
Novelette

Molto sostenuto

ped. simile

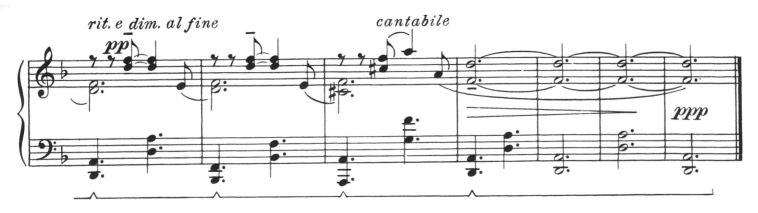

26
Etude

Allegro

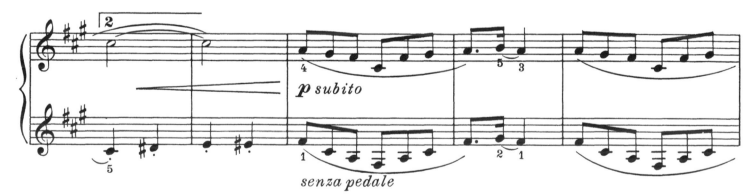

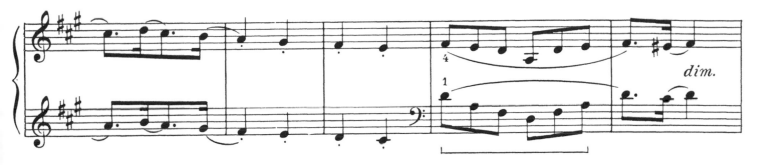

27
Dance

Moderato scherzando

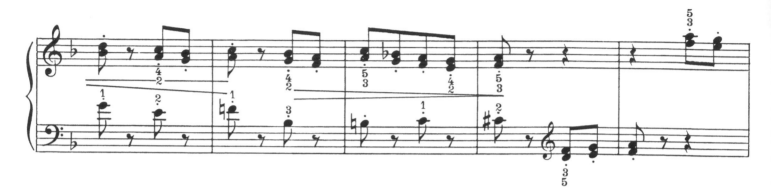

un poco rit.   a tempo

cresc. ed accel.

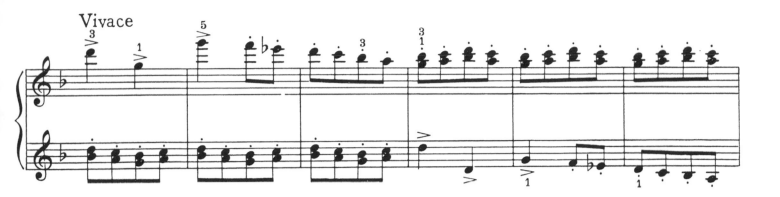

46334

28
Caprice

Andantino

poco a poco cresc.

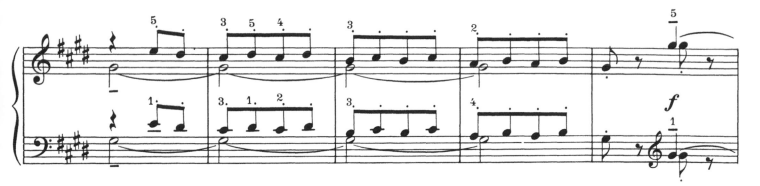

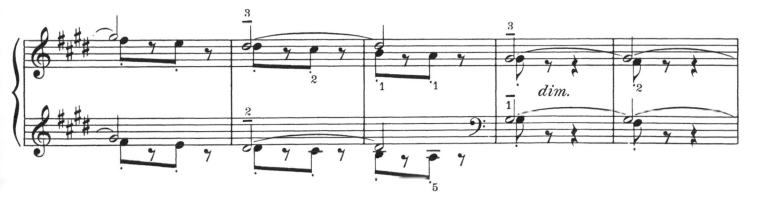

46334

29
Song of the Cavalry

Allegro molto

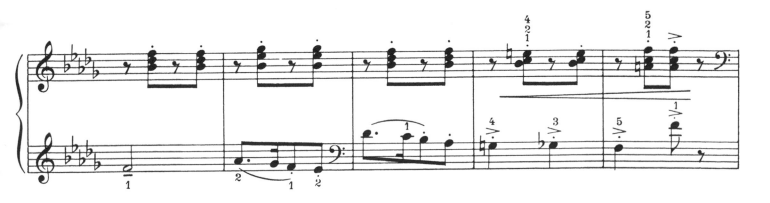

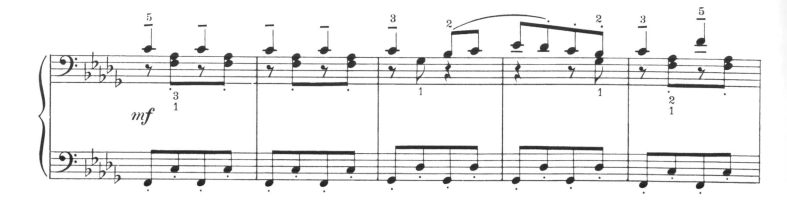

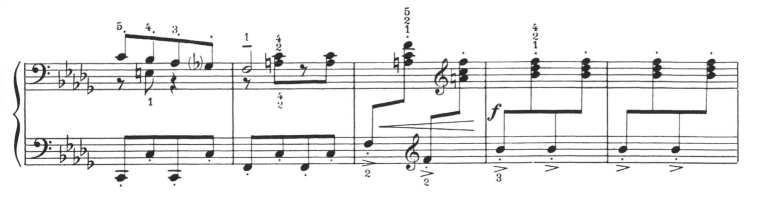

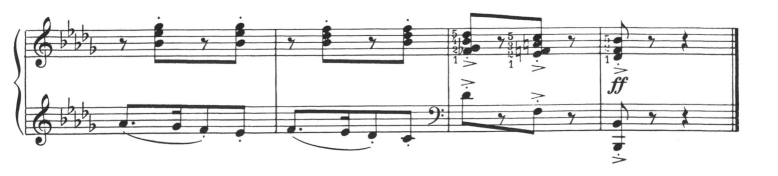

30
Dramatic Episode

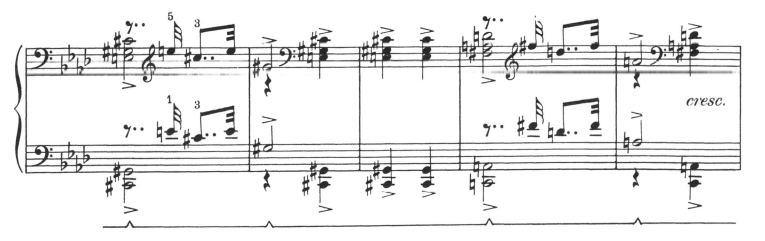